"The best thing
for being sad is
to learn something.
You may miss your father,
your mother, your dog,
your only love.
There's only one thing
for all of it. Learn!"

MERLIN TO ARTHUR,
CAMELOT

HYPERION

N E W Y O R K

• • •

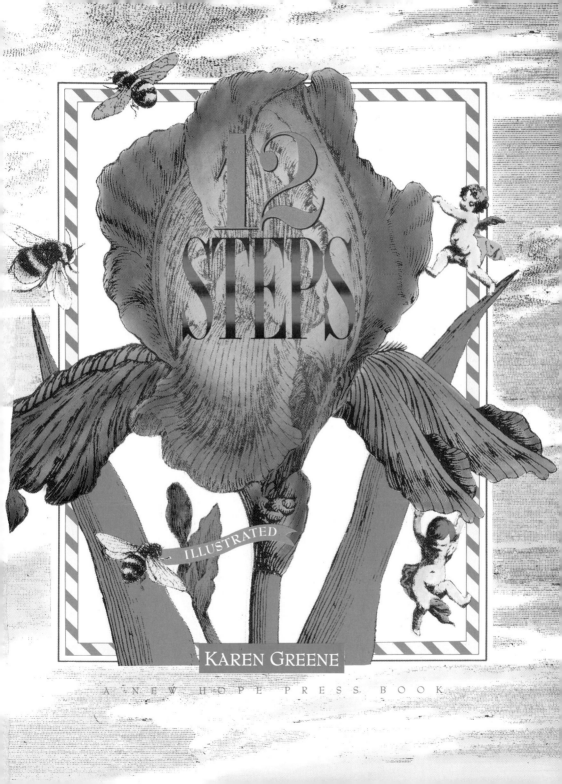

12 STEPS

ILLUSTRATED

KAREN GREENE

A NEW HOPE PRESS BOOK

*Many thanks to the Best and Greatest Artist, and the bountiful spirit
who once was named Frank Buchman. Gratitude and good wishes go with
each copy of this book to Anna Marie Heinz and to my dear Donovan,
as well as Peggy Ott, Gwen Ziesel, Maude, Pete, Serena, Chris Marshall,
Marge and Lee Hervey, Moral Re-Armament and Alcoholics Anonymous
World Services, Inc.*

Grateful acknowledgment is made to the following for
permission to reprint previously published material:
Helmers & Howard Publishers, Colorado Springs, Co., for
excerpts from *On the Tail of a Comet* by Garth Lean;
Macmillan Publishing Company, for an excerpt from *Fireflies*
by Rabindranath Tagore. Copyright 1928 by Macmillan Publishing
Company, renewed 1955 by Rabindranath Tagore;
Alcoholics Anonymous World Services, Inc., for permission
to reprint and adapt the Twelve Steps. The acknowledgment
regarding the Twelve Steps on page 32 forms an integral
part of this copyright notice.

Library of Congress Cataloging-In-Publication Data: Greene, Karen. 12 Steps
Illustrated/Karen Greene. p. cm. ISBN 1-56282-999-8 $12.95.
1. Conduct of life. 2. Twelve-step programs. 3. Buchman, Frank Nathan
Daniel, 1908-1961. I. Title. II. Title: Twelve Steps Illustrated.
BF637.C5G72 1991 362.29'186−dc20 91-19150 CIP

10 9 8 7 6 5 4 3 2 1
First Edition

To Edna, my
grandmother, and
Laura, my sister,
whose lives were altered
forever by alcoholic drivers.
Though they have faced
immense physical pain
and loss of freedom, two
more courageous people
could not be found
in all the world.

S pirituality, our lonesome voyage into the light of Oneness, is a secret kingdom of eternal curiosity to us. Today, everyone from the quantum mechanic to the cop on the beat puzzles over the meaning of life. We who would fathom what makes the universe go round must first go within, for it is now whispered by physicist and philosopher alike that this is where worlds begin.

The Twelve Steps may appear a humble vehicle, but they invite us to wander the infinite cosmos of inner space. They are the primary component of a program M. Scott Peck has called "without doubt, the single most effective agency of human transformation in our society."

Word for word, they are purely an empty vessel, for until we pour our dreams and determination into the Twelve Steps, we cannot drink from them. They are not a self-help plan, as they rely on a force endlessly greater than the individual. Don't mistake them for mantras, or kindly prayers calling for a perfect world. There is more to the Twelve Steps than at first meets even the mind's eye.

The philosophy that fathered the Steps was not designed to conquer addiction, the widest purpose to which it is presently being put. It grew in the heart of a small-town clergyman with a giant intent: He wished to remake the world spiritually.

We cannot say if the Twelve Steps might accomplish that, but they have become a kind of looking glass which reflects insights to millions who seek repair of a fragmented self-image. The repetitive form employed in the Twelve Steps implies that our own character is forever under construction.

The particular wording of the sentences was not finalized until 1938 drew to a close, though the concepts had been for three years the marrow of a fellowship group formed in New York City by two alcoholics, Dr. Bob Smith and Bill Wilson. Having often called themselves "a bunch of nameless alcoholics," the membership took for itself the scarcely more formal title of Alcoholics Anonymous.

A faithful serendipity seems to shepherd the Twelve Step philosophy. In an official biography, *Alcoholics Anonymous Comes of Age*, and in a memoir by Wilson's wife, *Lois Remembers*, we learn that New York physician William Silkworth, "a benign little doctor who loved drunks," intrigued Bill Wilson with the theory that his desperate condition was the equivalent of a physical allergy, coupled with a mental obsession. Abstinence was the obvious cure for the allergy, but Wilson said the ideas that became a treatment for the obsession – the Twelve Steps – were gathered "straight from the Oxford Groups and directly from Sam Shoemaker…and from nowhere else."

Samuel Shoemaker was the Princeton-educated pastor of Calvary Church in New York's Gramercy Park. He was also for a time the American leader of the international Oxford Group movement, and it was in attending Oxford meetings at the church that Wilson found lasting sobriety after two decades of progressive alcoholism. The Oxford Group was the creation of Frank Buchman, a thunderously energetic Lutheran minister from Allentown, Pa., who became a reputed missionary in India and Asia. The Oxford name was an informal title taken from the site in Britain of the group's first sizable gatherings.

B uchman advocated that the world could not change for the better until its citizens did. His philosophy arose from a universal wisdom he saw as the property of all people. The Bible and the lives of the early saints, particularly St. Augusteran, provided his strongest inspiration, along with Greek philosophers and such turn-of-the-century theologians as Robert Speer and Yale professor Henry Wright.

Oxford Group principles centered on absolute standards of behavior proposed in the Sermon on the Mount: absolute honesty, purity, selflessness and love. Group members did not pursue these with the holier-than-thou air one might expect. Buchman's insight that "faith is easier caught than taught" encouraged a genial, exuberant spirit among his followers that proved highly contagious.

Buchman repeatedly said he did not believe standards required rules, and he thought religions erred in telling people how to act. He saw the "absolutes" as a practical ruler against which both novice and seasoned believer could measure their own thoughts and behavior. He synthesized a plan of individual responsibility and spiritual independence that remains the foundation of AA today.

Silkworth counseled Wilson and Smith to avoid the absolutes in their group work, as he thought such rugged standards would frighten alcoholics. He urged them to first convey the critical nature of the alcoholic's physical condition, then follow with other key Oxford precepts:

- When facing trouble, admit that alone you are licked.
- Be honest with yourself.
- Confess your defects to someone else in confidence.
- Make restitution to those whom you've harmed.
- Give to others with no idea of reward.
- Commune each day with whatever God you believe in – and have the courage to listen.
- Be willing to obey the guidance received. Offer not only your life but your will to God.
- Continue these practices in all areas of your life.

"It was as simple and as mysterious as that," Wilson said. The ideas looked like novas in a night sky to AA's first members. The fusion of the individual will with "something greater than self" was the single star by which they would now steer a course. As Buchman noted, it was an idea at least two thousand years old.

Parallel concepts from contemporary sources confirmed the promise of the path that would be called the Twelve Steps. An alcoholic acquaintance of Wilson had turned for help to the great Swiss psychoanalyst, Carl Jung. Jung conveyed, from his clinical experience, that the only way to conquer an addiction permanently was through the substitution of a spiritual experience. By spirituality, Jung added, he did not simply mean conventional religion. (The acquaintance found his spiritual experience – and sobriety – through the Oxford Group.)

Wilson concurrently discovered the work of English psychologist William James. In a masterwork, *Varieties of Religious Experience,* James called self-surrender "the vital turning point" in the life of the soul. He defined it as "the throwing of our conscious selves on the mercy of powers which, whatever they may be, are more ideal than we are actually, and make for our redemption."

Twelve Step principles fostered not only this first healing of fractured symmetry, but also helped addicts maintain and expand inner health. Here was a plan for the lifelong care and fitness of the spiritual muscles.

More than fifty years later, Twelve Step programs are a circle of recovery for millions of individuals in an expanding universe of mutual support groups. Alcoholics Anonymous, Adult Children of Alcoholics, Overeaters Anonymous, Gamblers Anonymous and Narcotics Anonymous address but the tip of an iceberg of addictions. It is today estimated that in a given week, 15 to 20 million people attend one of the more than 500,000 addiction-recovery support groups modeled on AA in America. AA is active in over 100 other countries, as well.

The Twelve Steps are again being called to purposes other than addiction. They are easily recognizable in a practice called Mastermind Meditation, taught through Unity churches across the United States as a discipline to achieving life goals. Step Eleven has often been employed to incorporate life goals in Twelve Step work, as it has in this edition. The Minnesota-based Institute for Christian Living fashioned a Twelve Step program designed to help members "live with greater integrity."

Samuel Shoemaker felt there was probably no field of human endeavor for which the Twelve Steps wouldn't prove helpful. How or why they can do this we don't know, for their measure can't be found in the calculations of science.

T he Steps have a simplicity and fusion of purpose accessible to people of remarkably varied faiths, cultures and education levels. Their repetitive order outlines a gentle but persistent path toward self-understanding and positive action.

Scientists suspect that our experiences shape not only our beliefs, but the very circuitry of our brain cells. We can't simply wish away destructive tendencies. Character change comes through action – choosing behavior and emotional responses that appear to chemically alter or expand pathways in the brain.

There are some who say the Twelve Steps are *too* simple to achieve the results that have been credited to them. Recent decades were a time of such brilliant technical progress that inner wisdom was regarded as naive, even peculiar. But empirical science has ceased to casually toss aside the spirit, and theorists admit there are corners of conscious life closed to a completely mathematical approach. How do we "prove" a theory that time may run simultaneously backward and forward in a black hole in space?

The quest for the smallest or "ultimate" particle has literally come up empty. Each time science thought it had come to the bottom of matter, the bottom turned out to be a false one. All we have considered solid and separated is now classified as an unbroken web of radiant energy, blinking in and out of existence. Physicist and metaphysicist cross paths at the corner of a wondrous question: Is the true universe the one we cannot see?

The equations have become so complicated that only a handful of scientists understands them, yet the great theme of physics today is the search for patterns of simplicity and symmetry. Mathematicians and physicists say that a very simple theory often proves most aesthetic – and correct. "Beauty" is counted as the premier guide to the dominion of truth.

There is loose talk of God again among the great stargazers, as there was in the time of Copernicus, who was filled with awe for "the Best and Greatest Artist." (Einstein made God safe for modern science with the famous, lyrical sentence: "I want to know His thoughts, the rest are details.") Once more come hints from cosmology's quarters of an interconnectedness, a single-mindedness, that permeates all matter.

The scattered galaxies were once a single entity, and perhaps human consciousness was, as well. Great distances isolate Earth and her moon, yet the two are startlingly capable of affecting one another. May the same possibly be true of men poised at opposite ends of Earth?

Does an elegant, unified energy imprint and order all that exists for ultimate good? Are the Twelve Steps a kind of touchstone enabling this creative energy – His energy – to express symmetry in our individual lives?

We don't need quantum theory to trace some tangible elements that make Twelve Step work rewarding.

Frank Buchman had an instinct for the strength found in human fellowship, well before modern society spawned a corrosive isolation among individuals and families. The Swiss psychiatrist Paul Tournier, among others, has credited Buchman and his movement with a considerable role in the history of group therapy.

Buchman conceived Oxford Group meetings as a nucleus of friendship. The earliest meetings were even called "house parties." They consisted of common people sharing life-changing experiences as a result of working with Oxford precepts. "People are more lastingly helped if you tell them of your faults than of your virtues," he said – and the concept is still the turning point of Twelve Step programs. Honesty, humility and empathy are qualities that flourish with Twelve Step work.

All sense of community, it is said, springs inevitably from cooperative rituals. Twelve Step programs bring communion not only with others, but also with our Higher Power. Both kinds of communion seem helpful to the self-surrender Carl Jung and William James spoke of, the letting go that creates a space which universal energies can occupy. The Twelve Steps gently bring to light the bankruptcy of the vast human illusion of external power, and point out how very naked is the emperor who searches for a sense of completeness outside himself – whether his "new clothes" are material goods, relationships or an alphabet of mind-altering substances. The Twelve Steps champion quite a different tale: True power generates from a Higher Power, then radiates to us in proportion to the magnitude of our faith and self-surrender.

Addicts are not expected to wed themselves to willpower – the "Just say no" approach. They are asked to open to something infinitely more long-lived than individual will – to be willing to align with what cosmologists have called "the listening Universe."

S piritual journeys are commonly launched with a longing that our lives might magically change. The journey progresses only when we perceive that the pilot puts right his drift, not the sky or the stars. The doors to each Step open one way – inward. There is no Step suited to blaming environment or other beings. A popular Twelve Step slogan echoes the Buddhist tenet that we cannot change anything or anyone but ourselves, though once we do that, all will change around us.

We come full circle to Frank Buchman's great notion that the world will not change until we do. Toward the end of his life, he suggested that not only his own time was running out: "It is no longer a question of whether we must change," he said, "but simply how."

One of the most controversial scientific views emerging is that no "observations" exist independent of the observer. This would include all visual aspects of nature, as well as her "laws." Our representation of reality is, for us, the only reality, since external life may function as a mirror or metaphor of our inner perceptions.

Physics waltzes for the moment with metaphysics, to the graceful theory that belief both precedes and creates our experience. "Believing is seeing" may be far more effective spiritual software than the familiar "seeing is believing."

"The soul *is* the world," proclaimed the German mystic Meister Eckhart, over 700 years before "You create your own reality" became a metaphysical anthem. As unfamiliar as these quantum realms may feel to some of us, the Twelve Step philosophy is quite at home there.

I t could be quite important to position Twelve Step work in the verbal here and now. Our point of power, from which we have ability to act, is not operational in the past or future. A focus ♦ ♦ ♦ on the present encourages us to "see" our goals moving into existence – a kind of creative self-deception that psychologists now consider the hallmark of a healthy mind. Positive mental rituals, through a chemical process we haven't quite mapped, are now thought the most effective way to work the clay of cells and self.

The idea has been clothed in a bright wardrobe of modern disciplines with syllable-rich names like psychoneuroimmunology (the idea that optimism boosts our immune system and pessimism depresses it). Neurolinguistic programming (NLP) employs language – and its powerful access to our internal perceptions – as an eloquent tool in behavior modification. Springing from the notion that specific words call up worlds within us, NLP echoes the work of Maxwell Maltz, popularizer of psychocybernetics, or psychologist Rollo May, who both have suggested that imagination serves a higher purpose than artifice. They see it not only as the prelude to the creative act, but to every human action.

In *The Courage to Create,* May predicts that imagination will one day be seen as our shortest passage to the source of all being. He adds that in the half-lost language of myth and legend, a subconscious wisdom acquired over thousands of generations, deliverance from evil invariably comes through the imagination.

In his latest work, *The Cry for Myth,* May heralds the complement to reason – the "mythic language of color and imagination." The absence of these elements, he says, may partly account for high rates of addiction and teen suicide, as well as a profound confusion of lust with love.

The theorist Max Luscher has called color "the mother tongue of the unconscious." Kahlil Gibran spoke of art as "a step on the way from Nature to eternity." The Greeks proposed that the appreciation of beauty itself was an inevitable path to truth. Plato envisioned that one day we would have but "a single science, which is the science of beauty everywhere."

This edition is a postage-stamp playground of image, color and word, created to suggest a wider frame for Twelve Step work. If some images appear to have wandered in from a work of children's literature, it is not without invitation. Carl Jung urged us to locate the "wonder child" within – calling it "all that is abandoned and exposed and at the same time, divinely powerful." John Bradshaw, in *Homecoming: Reclaiming and Championing Your Inner Child,* suggests that the wonder child is the very center of our spirituality and "the part of you that bears a likeness to your creator."

All endeavors with these twelve simple sentences are artistic, for they serve as a canvas on which we can create, with the inspiration of the "Best and Greatest Artist," a life closer to our heart's desire. The Twelve Steps conduct us to the crossroads of imagination and self-understanding, to a corner where mind not only meets matter, but is all that matters.

"The future," Frank Buchman said, "depends not upon what others decide to do, but upon what you decide to become." In this spirit, the Twelve Steps deliver us beyond the dream of flight, to the moment of flight. They ask that we not only admire beauty, but manifest it.

"What saves a man is to take a step. Then another step. It is always the same step, but you have to take it," wrote Antoine de Saint Exupéry.

When you take the Twelve Steps, you walk toward the light within you. Drawing upon the light, day after day, you design a greater self. In time, all wandering artists step into the limitless kingdom, into the service of something greater than self. ◆ ◆ ◆

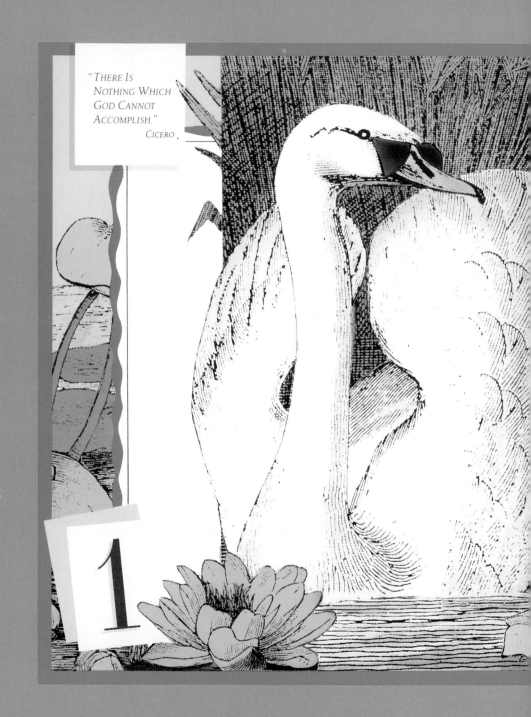

"THERE IS
NOTHING WHICH
GOD CANNOT
ACCOMPLISH."
CICERO

1

My
life is not the
life I long for.
I now know that
on my own
I am powerless
to change it
for the better.

THE LORD IS MY SHEPHERD

2

I have
come to believe that there is
a great force in the
universe that will work for
my benefit if I but ask.

"IN THE
LAST ANALYSIS,
SOMEHOW OR OTHER,
THERE MUST BE A SINGLE
ENERGY OPERATING IN THE WORLD."
PIERRE TEILHARD DE CHARDIN

WILLIAM WORDSWORTH

"LIFE IS GOD'S NOVEL.
LET HIM WRITE IT."
ISAAC BASHEVIS SINGER

3

believe & soar

I now
decide to turn my
will and my life over to
my Higher Power.

I become honest about myself as never before. With Truth and Courage as my companions, I take a complete moral inventory.

the light within

"PRINCES AND LORDS
ARE BUT THE
BREATH OF KINGS,
AN HONEST MAN'S
THE NOBLEST
WORK OF GOD."
ROBERT BURNS

L5

I admit
to my Higher Power, to
myself and to another person
the nature of my mistakes
and faults of personality.

HAPPINESS IS A DECISION

"EXAMPLE IS NOT
THE MAIN THING IN
INFLUENCING OTHERS.
IT'S THE ONLY THING."
ALBERT SCHWEITZER

16

ASK & YOU SHALL RECEIVE

I form
a true desire
for my Higher
Power to remove
my faults
forever.

"ALL THINGS BY IMMORTAL POWER,
NEAR OR FAR, HIDDENLY
TO EACH OTHER LINKED ARE,
THAT THOU CANST NOT STIR A FLOWER
WITHOUT TROUBLING OF A STAR."
FRANCIS THOMPSON

"GOD IS THE EAST
AND THE WEST,
AND WHEREVER
YE TURN, THERE
IS GOD'S FACE."
KORAN, 7TH CENTURY A.D.

I humbly
ask my
Higher Power
to remove my
faults forever.

7

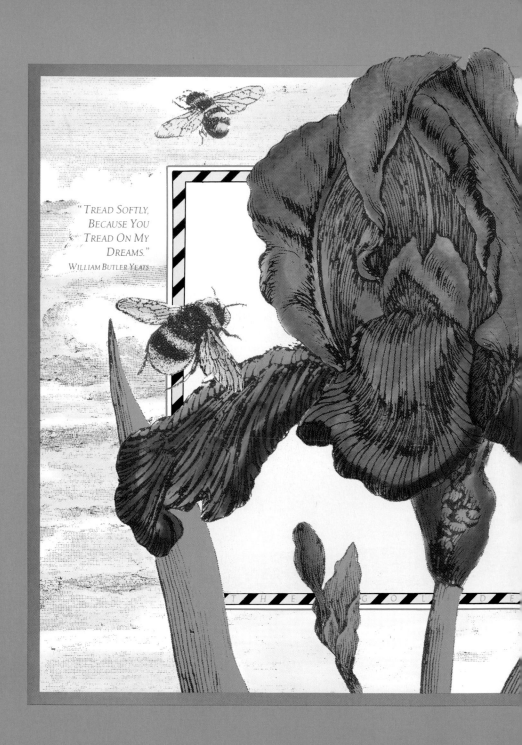

"TREAD SOFTLY,
BECAUSE YOU
TREAD ON MY
DREAMS."
WILLIAM BUTLER YEATS

I list
all those
persons I have
hurt or harmed
and state my
desire to make
amends to them.

8

"FAITH IS THE BIRD THAT FEELS THE LIGHT A

TRUE

I make
amends to
persons I have
hurt or harmed
where it is possible.

WIN

ND SINGS WHEN

WISHES

THE DAWN IS STILL DARK."

HAVE

GS

9

RABINDRANATH TAGORE

With
Truth and Courage
as my companions,
I commit to taking
a continuous
moral inventory.

THE POINT OF POWER

"BE CARELES
IF YOU MUST, BU

I do not hesitate
to admit when
my thoughts,
words or actions
are wrong.

YOUR DRESS
EP A TIDY SOUL."
MARK TWAIN

10

IS IN THE PRESENT

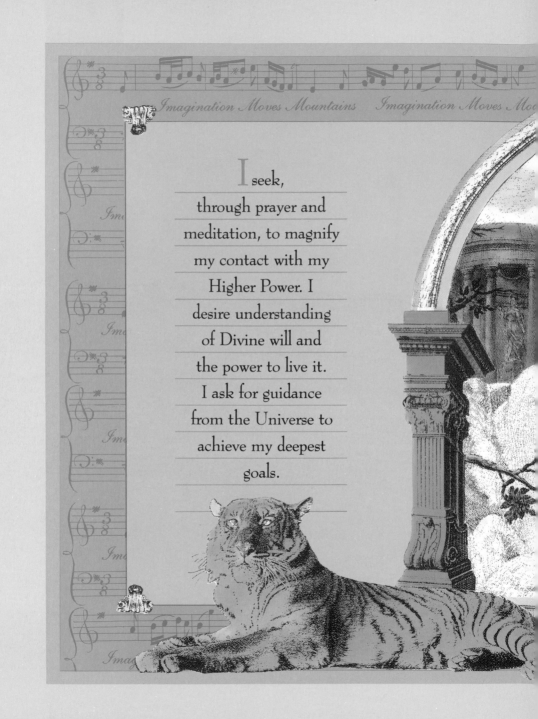

I seek, through prayer and meditation, to magnify my contact with my Higher Power. I desire understanding of Divine will and the power to live it. I ask for guidance from the Universe to achieve my deepest goals.

"IF YOUR PRAYER
IS SINCERE...YOU
WILL UNDERSTAND
THAT PRAYER IS
AN EDUCATION."
FEODOR DOSTOEVSKI

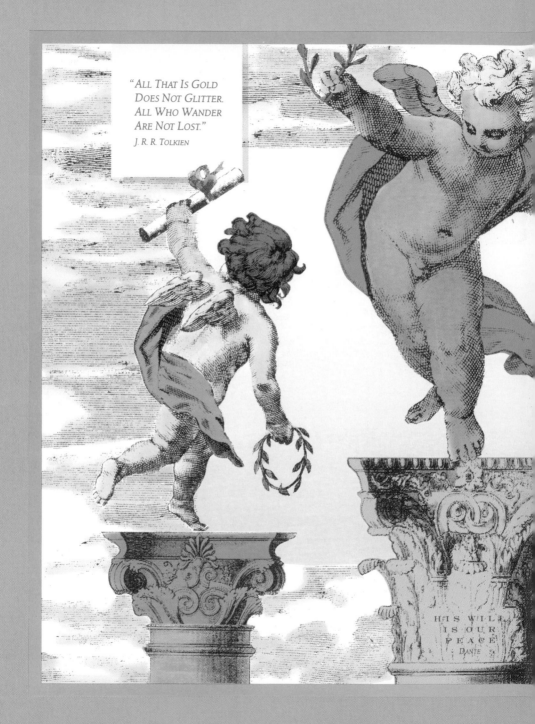

"ALL THAT IS GOLD
DOES NOT GLITTER.
ALL WHO WANDER
ARE NOT LOST."

J. R. R. TOLKIEN

HIS WILL
IS OUR
PEACE DANTE

I begin each day's journey with great joy and expectation of the bounty that awaits me. In thanks for my soul's awakening, I share this message with others and I practice these principles in all my affairs.

12

The man of whom that was written is barely remembered now, yet the first footsteps of the phenomenon that is the Twelve Step movement can still be found in the faded imprint of an equally remarkable movement he founded, the Oxford Group.

Only one full biography exists of Frank Buchman, *On the Tail of a Comet,* but author Garth Lean required over 500 pages to tell the stirring history of a man with heroic energy and faith, called "a modern Francis of Assisi." Buchman's influence and success kindled great envy, however, and he endured venomous opposition during a long career.

Born in Pennsburg, Pa., this small-town clergyman's powerful missionary work in China, India and Europe carried him to the highest levels of international society. Buchman counseled royalty, presidents and prime ministers, as well as major business, political and labor officials of his day—a circle which ranged from Harry Truman to Gandhi.

Oxford Group meetings drew astonishing crowds: 25,000 on a single day in Copenhagen in 1935; 25,000 over three days in Birmingham, England, in July of 1936; 100,000 over two days in the Netherlands in 1937. More than 30,000 people packed the Hollywood Bowl one night in July of 1939, and another 15,000 were turned away—a rally said to have inspired the Frank Capra film, *Meet John Doe.* During these years,

PHOTO – ARTHUR STRONG

thousands of unpaid Oxford Group "associates" escorted the message across the globe. In 1934, Dr. Bob Smith and Bill Wilson heard the Oxford principles that enabled them to conquer alcoholism and later launch AA.

Complaints from a vocal minority within Oxford University led Buchman to re-name the movement in 1938, to Moral Re-Armament (MRA). The name signified Buchman's foreboding that if humankind did not arm spiritually, the absence of guidance would lead to worldwide conflict. With encouragement from Mrs. Henry Ford, a Moral Re-Armament center opened in 1942 on Mackinac Island in Michigan. Here, those who led the various MRA global missions were trained.

A Norwegian artist, Victor Sparr, recalled that, "It was a free life led by an invisible mysterious force…each and all followed the inner voice, with no fixed jobs, no salaries, no chains of command."

Buchman had little tolerance for red tape or institutions and scorned "movement mindedness." Followers who asked him for specific advice on a course of action were admonished to "do anything God lets you!"

By the summer of 1943, over 2,000 business and labor leaders from around the world had come to Mackinac Island to learn MRA concepts. With the professional help of supporters in the Hollywood entertainment community, the ideology was translated into many theatrical plays, eventually seen by audiences on every continent. A full-length color film of one play, *Freedom,* was said to inspire the first productive meeting between Arkansas Governor Orville Faubus and a representative of the NAACP during the most violent time of school desegregation in the South, a meeting later characterized on CBS radio as "possibly the most significant news event of 1959."

As a result of immense Oxford and MRA work in Europe prior to

World War II, Buchman has been partly credited for the selflessness shown by the people of England and Scandinavia throughout years of deprivation.

In 1946, an MRA headquarters opened in Caux, Switzerland, to enable those from the war-divided countries of Europe to meet in a conciliatory atmosphere. Buchman spent his remaining years working there with statesmen and leaders, such as Konrad Adenauer of Germany, to heal the wounds of World War II. In much of this, he was checkmated by the rise of Communism. Though at times disheartened, he prophetically told his followers that Communism would be "a spent force" within their lives.

The Caux meetings became a cultural bazaar, drawing observers from around the world. A delegation of Buddhist abbots traveled all the way from Burma to hear "the man who comes only once in a thousand years."

The minister who preached that, "Peace is people becoming different," received two Nobel Peace Prize nominations and decorations from eight governments before he died in 1961. *The New York Times* and *The Los Angeles Times* placed Buchman's obituary on Page One.

Some found him a curious spiritual figure. He was full of determination, yet given to fits of laughter. He was immeasurably brash at times, but a brilliant listener, with candor and compassion for all. The words that might capture Buchman best belong to Walt Whitman. In *Leaves of Grass* he celebrated the large soul of America, saying, "Here is the hospitality which forever indicates heroes."

One enigma endures. The small-town clergyman called "a turning point in the history of the modern world" by the Archbishop of Vienna is almost forgotten. But celebrity is not proof of the power of a particular idea, and if fame has not pursued Buchman of late, he did not seek it in life. His only wish was "to awaken the possibilities that are within men."

By this measure Buchman's shadow is long, and lengthens each time the Twelve Steps are whispered by someone who has never known his name.

◆ ◆ ◆

TWELVE STEPS OF AA

1. We admitted we were powerless over alcohol – that our lives had become unmanageable.
2. Came to believe that a Power greater than ourselves could restore us to sanity.
3. Made a decision to turn our will and our lives over to the care of God *as we understood Him*.
4. Made a searching and fearless moral inventory of ourselves.
5. Admitted to God, to ourselves, and to another human being the exact nature of our wrongs.
6. Were entirely ready to have God remove these defects of character.
7. Humbly asked Him to remove our shortcomings.
8. Made a list of all persons we had harmed, and became willing to make amends to them all.
9. Made direct amends to such people wherever possible, except when to do so would injure them or others.
10. Continued to take personal inventory, and when we were wrong promptly admitted it.
11. Sought through prayer and meditation to improve our conscious contact with God *as we understood Him*, praying only for knowledge of His will for us and the power to carry that out.
12. Having had a spiritual awakening as the result of these steps, we tried to carry the message to other alcoholics and to practice these principles in all our affairs.

◆ ◆ ◆

"You can make
a fresh start
with your
final breath."

BERTOLT BRECHT